YOU MUST REMEMBER THIS

1972

MILESTONES, MEMORIES,
TRIVIA AND FACTS, NEWS EVENTS,
PROMINENT PERSONALITIES &
SPORTS HIGHLIGHTS OF THE YEAR

TO :

FROM :

MESSAGE :

selected and researched
by
betsy dexter

WARNER Ⓦ TREASURES ™

PUBLISHED BY WARNER BOOKS

A TIME WARNER COMPANY

COPYRIGHT ©1995
by Betsy Dexter
All Rights Reserved.

Warner Books, Inc.
1271 Avenue of the Americas
New York, New York 10020

Warner Treasures is a
trademark of Warner Books, Inc.

A Time Warner Company

DESIGN:
CAROL BOKUNIEWICZ DESIGN
PRINTED IN SINGAPORE
FIRST PRINTING : MAY 1995
10 9 8 7 6 5 4 3 2 1
ISBN : 0-446-91049-X

DEMOCRATIC NATIONAL COMMITTEE

It was the year President Richard Nixon was reelected by one of the greatest landslides since FDR's in 1936. Only Massachusetts and the District of Columbia voted for Democrat George McGovern, whose campaign was hampered when running mate Thomas Eagleton, a senator from Missouri, was replaced by Sargent Shriver after it was revealed Eagleton had been treated for manic depression. A bungled burglary by 5 men caught in Democratic National Headquarters—in the Washington apartment complex called **WATERGATE**—had no effect on the president's reelection effort.

In a landmark decision, the Supreme Court declared the death penalty "cruel and unusual punishment" and ruled it unconstitutional.

'72

In March, the Equal Rights Amendment, prohibiting sex discrimination against women, was approved by Congress and sent to the states for ratification.

In November, 500 angry Native Americans seized control of the Bureau of Indian Affairs building in Washington, DC, to protest the government's continuing history of broken promises.

newsreel

GOVERNOR GEORGE WALLACE WAS SHOT WHILE CAMPAIGNING FOR PRESIDENT IN LAUREL, MARYLAND, AND WAS LEFT PARALYZED FROM THE WAIST DOWN. GUNMAN ARTHUR BREMER HAD BEEN STALKING WALLACE FOR MONTHS. WALLACE CONTINUED HIS NATIONWIDE CAMPAIGN FROM A WHEELCHAIR.

Responding to a spate of hijackings, TWA and American Airlines announced they would begin inspecting passengers' baggage before they boarded the airplane.

In the Philippines, President **ferdinand marcos** imposed martial law and arrested hundreds of Filipinos as Communist subversives.

headlines

international

In Londonderry, Northern Ireland, when British troops fired on illegal Catholic protesters, 13 were killed in what came to be known as the "Derry Massacre." Great Britain subsequently imposed direct rule over Northern Ireland and suspended its government.

Ceylon declared itself an independent republic and changed its name to Sri Lanka.

In February, President Richard Nixon became the first U.S. chief of state to visit mainland China. The trip ended with a joint agreement to work toward the normalization of relations. In May, Nixon became the first American president to set foot in Moscow. Subsequent meetings resulted in a strategic arms pact between the two superpowers.

A burgeoning business in sex therapy swept the country. Hundreds of clinics appeared coast to coast. Treatment most often involved removing couples to hotels to escape daily worries. **THE CENSUS BUREAU REVEALED THAT THE UNITED STATES HAD REACHED A BIRTHRATE THAT ALLOWED FOR SUB-ZERO POPULATION GROWTH.** Emphasis was put on kissing and touching nonerogenous zones. With less importance placed on intercourse, according to experts, problems surrounding the act would fade away. For citizens who needed stronger medicine, Johns Hopkins University offered sex-change operations. The facility announced that, as of this year, it had performed 500 such procedures. Doctors claimed there were roughly 7,500 would-be transsexuals in the United States, most of them men wanting to be women.

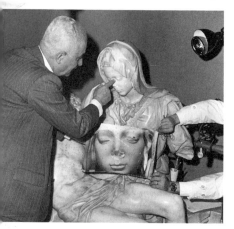

Insisting that he was Jesus Christ, a man in Italy attacked Michelangelo's sculpture *The Pietà* with a hammer. The assailant, Laszlo Toth, shattered the head and arm of the statue of the Virgin Mary. It was restored and placed in a shatterproof glass case.

gloria steinem,

the nation's premier feminist, established *Ms.* magazine.

THE FIRST WOMAN RABBI IN THE UNITED STATES, SALLY PRIESAND, WAS ORDAINED IN CINCINNATI, OHIO.

cultural
milestones

timesavers

A TEXAS INSTRUMENTS POCKET CALCULATOR. Price: $119.50.

A NEW ANSWERING MACHINE that answered on the first ring, gave and recorded messages, and boasted the optional AC/DC or battery. The price: $139.50.

television

**top-rated
tv shows
of the
1972 season:**

1. "All in the Family" (CBS)

2. "The Flip Wilson Show" (NBC)

3. "Marcus Welby, M.D." (ABC)

4. "Gunsmoke" (CBS)

5. "The ABC Movie of the Week" (ABC)

6. "Sanford and Son" (NBC)

7. "Mannix" (CBS)

8. "Funny Face" (tie) (CBS)

9. "Adam l2" (tie) (NBC)

10. "The Mary Tyler Moore Show" (tie) (CBS)

11. "Here's Lucy" (tie) (CBS)

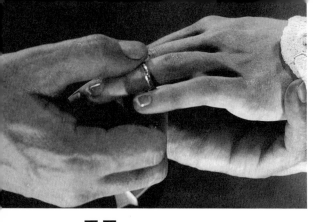

milestones

notable weddings

Gordon Cooper, 45, the angry young man of the original Project Mercury team of astronauts, who left the space program in 1970 after two earth orbital missions, when NASA banned him from sports car racing, to **Susan Taylor,** 26, a former schoolteacher, on a houseboat in Miami Beach on May 6.

DAVID BRINKLEY, 51, SOURPUSS "NBC NEWS" COMMENTATOR, AND **SUSAN ADOLPH,** 32, FORMER WIFE OF A FLORIDA LAWYER, IN WILLIAMSBURG, VA.

'72

D E A T H S

Mahalia Jackson, gospel singer, died on January 27 at 60.

Marianne Moore, poet, died on February 5.

Walter Winchell, columnist and broadcaster, died on February 20.

J. Edgar Hoover, head of the FBI since 1924, died on May 2 at 77.

Howard Johnson, founder of orange-roofed restaurant chain, died on June 20.

Oscar Levant, musician, legendary wit, and neurotic personality, died on August 15.

Ezra Pound, poet, died on November 1 at 80.

births

CHRISTINA APPLEGATE, actress and star of "Married . . . With Children," was born on November 25 in Los Angeles.

ALYSSA MILANO of TV's "Who's the Boss?" was born on December 19 in New York City.

JOE MCINTYRE, founding member of super-group New Kids on the Block, was born on December 31 in Needham, MA.

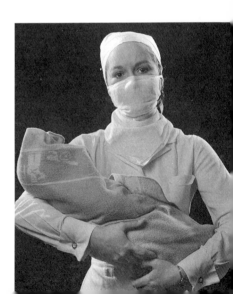

1. **the first time ever i saw your face** Roberta Flack
2. **alone again (naturally)** Gilbert O'Sullivan
3. **american pie** Don McLean
4. **without you** Nilsson
5. **i can see clearly now** Johnny Nash
6. **a horse with no name** America
7. **baby, don't get hooked on me** Mac Davis
8. **me and mrs. jones** Billy Paul
9. **the candy man** Sammy Davis, Jr.
10. **lean on me** Bill Withers

'72
hit music

ROBERT MOOG, an engineer, patented the Moog synthesizer, an electronic musical instrument that could duplicate the sounds of various instruments with remarkable accuracy. It soon became all the rage with "progressive" rock and rollers.

SINGER **HELEN REDDY** CAUSED A FEMINIST SENSATION WITH HER RECORDING OF "I AM WOMAN."

bette midler
released *The Divine Miss M.*, an album that revived songs from the previous 40 years.

12

13

bestselling

fiction

1. **the winds of war**
   herman wouk
2. **the exorcist**
   william peter blatty
3. **the day of the jackal**
   frederick forsyth
4. **wheels**
   arthur hailey
5. **the word**
   irving wallace
6. **captains and kings**
   taylor caldwell
7. **message from malaga**
   helen macinnes
8. **my name is asher lev**
   chaim potok
9. **rabbit redux**
   john updike
10. **the terminal man**
    michael crichton

14

books

HEINRICH BOLL
WON THE NOBEL PRIZE
FOR LITERATURE.

THE OLYMPIC GAMES IN MUNICH

turned tragic when Arab terrorists gunned down 11 Israeli athletes. During a shootout with West German police, 5 terrorists and 9 more Israelis were killed. The games were further politicized when a pair of African-American athletes were banned from future Olympic competition for raising their fists in a Black Power salute on the victory stand after winning medals for the 400-yard dash. On a less controversial note, American Mark Spitz won a record 7 gold medals in swimming competitions.

IN TENNIS, THE U.S. TEAM WON THE DAVIS CUP FOR THE 5TH YEAR IN A ROW.

'72

Pittsburgh Pirate outfielder Roberto Clemente became the 11th player in baseball history to reach 3,000 base hits. After the season, Clemente died in a plane crash while trying to distribute food in his native Puerto Rico.

sports

THE DALLAS COWBOYS OBLITERATED THE MIAMI DOLPHINS 24–3 IN THE SUPER BOWL THE VICTORY WAS WORTH $15,000 TO EACH COWBOY.

In a much-discussed decision, the New York Court of Appeals upheld the right of a New York City woman to be a professional baseball umpire.

chess fever

swept the nation after Bobby Fischer defeated Boris Spassky of the USSR to win the World Chess Championship.

DIANA ROSS MADE HER LEADING LADY DEBUT IN *LADY SINGS THE BLUES*, A RENDERING OF THE LIFE OF BILLIE HOLIDAY.

Oscar winners for 1972 movies: **Marlon Brando** won for Best Actor in ***The Godfather,*** which also took Best Picture. *Cabaret* garnered Best Director for **Bob Fosse,** Best Actress for **Liza Minnelli,** and Best Supporting Actor for **Joel Grey.** Best Supporting Actress was the relatively little-known **Eileen Heckart** in *Butterflies Are Free.*

top ten box-office stars

1. Clint Eastwood
2. George C. Scott
3. Gene Hackman
4. John Wayne
5. Barbra Streisand
6. Marlon Brando
7. Paul Newman
8. Steve McQueen
9. Dustin Hoffman
10. Goldie Hawn

Joel Grey in Cabaret

IN WHAT WAS TO BECOME A MAJOR TREND OF THE SEVENTIES, IRWIN ALLEN WROTE AND PRODUCED **THE POSEIDON ADVENTURE,** THE FIRST OF A SERIES OF DISASTER MOVIES. THE GENRE PROVED TO BE A POPULAR FAVORITE.

box-office champs

1. *The Godfather* (Paramount) — $86,275,000
2. *The Poseidon Adventure* (20th Century-Fox) — $42,000,000
3. *What's Up, Doc?* (Warner Bros.) — $28,000,000
4. *Deliverance* (Warner Bros.) — $22,600,000
5. *Jeremiah Johnson* (Warner Bros.) — $21,900,000

movies

In one of the rawer efforts to ever hit the screen, Ralph Bakshi made **Fritz the Cat,** the world's first full-length X-rated cartoon.

19

'72

In 1972, Detroit faced a raft of complaints from new-car owners. Many new cars were hard to start, and many tended to miss and stall in traffic. According to auto makers, these problems were the result of newly enacted Federal

cars

Exhaust Emission Standards. But the Big Three auto manufacturers were faulted for trying to comply with these standards in the cheapest ways—modifying existing engines, rather than developing new ones.

CONSUMER REPORTS
MAGAZINE SINGLED OUT
THE FORD GRAN TORINO
AND THE MAZDA RX2
COUPE AS THE BEST BUYS
OF THE YEAR.

**A Mercedes Benz set upscale con-
sumers back from low-end $6,345
to an all-the-options $15,094.**

The watchwords in makeup were "warm" and "clear." Everyone wanted makeup that didn't look like makeup. **Short dresses** were de rigueur for evening get-togethers, combined with a fur blouson for style. **Shirtdresses** proved more popular than ever. Women favored more casual combos of shirt

fashion

and sweater over pants. By fall, **sweaters** stood out as the height of fashion, especially longer sweaters worn with skirts of luxuriant fabrics. **Silk** and **angora** were very In, and no coat could call itself decent without fur lining. Perhaps the biggest fashion breakthrough: Women were now seen in styles once reserved for men, such as cardigans over thin shirts for stepping out in the evening.

THOSE STAPLES OF THE MALE STYLE, **DOUBLE KNIT POLYESTER BELL-BOTTOMS,** SOLD FOR $16 A PAIR. **THE EVER-POPULAR SILK TIE** COST $7.50. **PANTYHOSE** WENT FOR $3.99.

final

factoid

life magazine, which had been published weekly for 36 years, suspended publication.

LIFE

MUGGING

A young
mugger
talks about
his 1,000 'hits'

How to avoid
an attacker,
what to do if
he moves in

**George
Plimpton
Hunts the
World's
Biggest
Elephant**

25

archive photos: inside front cover, pages 1, 10, 11, 15, 21, 22, 23, inside back cover.

associated press: pages 2, 5, 6, 7, 16, 17.

photofest: pages 9, 13, 18, 19.

album cover:
courtesy of rustyn birch

photo research:
alice albert

coordination:
rustyn birch

design:
carol bokuniewicz design
mutsumi hyuga

'72